AVIDYĀ

Vidyan Ravinthiran was born in Leeds, to Sri Lankan Tamils. His first book of poems, *Grun-tu-molani* (Bloodaxe Books, 2014), was shortlisted for the Forward Prize for Best First Collection, the Seamus Heaney Centre Poetry Prize and the Michael Murphy Memorial Prize. His second, *The Million-petalled Flower of Being Here* (Bloodaxe Books, 2019), won a Northern Writers' Award and was a Poetry Book Society Recommendation. It was shortlisted for the 2019 Forward Prize for Best Collection, the 2019 T.S. Eliot Prize and the 2021 Ledbury Munthe Poetry Prize for Second Collections. His third collection, *Avidyā*, was published by Bloodaxe in 2025. Vidyan Ravinthiran is co-editor with Seni Seneviratne and Shash Trevett of the anthology *Out of Sri Lanka: Tamil, Sinhala and English poetry from Sri Lanka and its diasporas* (Bloodaxe Books, 2023), a Poetry Book Society Special Commendation.

After teaching at the universities of Cambridge, Durham and Birmingham in the UK, he now teaches at Harvard in the US. He is the author of *Elizabeth Bishop's Prosaic* (Bucknell, 2015), winner of both the University English Prize and the Warren-Brooks Award for Outstanding Literary Criticism; a collection of essays, *Worlds Woven Together* (Columbia University Press, 2022); a critical study, *Spontaneity and Form in Modern Prose* (OUP, 2020); and *Asian/Other*, a fusion of poetry criticism and memoir (Icon Books, UK, & W.W. Norton, USA).

VIDYAN RAVINTHIRAN

Avidyā

BLOODAXE BOOKS

ISBN: 978 1 78037 739 1

First published 2025 by
Bloodaxe Books Ltd,
Eastburn,
South Park,
Hexham,
Northumberland NE46 1BS.

www.bloodaxebooks.com
For further information about Bloodaxe titles
please visit our website and join our mailing list
or write to the above address for a catalogue.

Supported using public funding by
**ARTS COUNCIL
ENGLAND**

Cover design: Neil Astley & Pamela Robertson-Pearce.

Printed in Great Britain by Bell & Bain Limited, 303 Burnfield Road,
Thornliebank, Glasgow G46 7UQ, Scotland, on acid-free paper
sourced from mills with FSC chain of custody certification.

There are four lights.

JEAN-LUC PICARD

There are no others.

RAMANA MAHARSHI

ACKNOWLEDGEMENTS

Some of these poems, or versions of them, appeared in *The American Scholar, Ars Notoria, The Australian Book Review, The Best American Poetry 2024, The Griffith Review, Gutter, The Harvard Review, HEAT* (Australia), *The Lily Poetry Review, The London Review of Books, Magma, The North, Poetry, Poetry London,* and *Walter de la Mare: Critical Appraisals.*

CONTENTS

As a

Sri
Lankan
Tamil

I feel strongly
about

three o'clock in the afternoon

Your demon's basic

dilemma's this
—as well as feeling all they hear
is either poison or their own

original thought,
otherness is something
they'll never get their heads around;

since they wish to eat people,
it must be—given half a chance—
those same people would eat them...

Leaving for home,
a goatherd told his scarecrow
to watch out and not just for thieves

but tigers and demons too:
with emphasis, he said
not *puli* and *muni* but *pulikili* and *munikini*

—tigerish tigers and demonic demons!
One of each,
creeping in the shade toward their prey,

heard this and were terrified
by word of a beast like them
in every way but raised to a new power;

the tiger ran off and the demon
disguised himself as one of the goats.
Which fooled nobody.

Least of all our heroes,
Able-Talker and the Strong-Armed One
here to make a sacrifice to Durgā.

One seized the demon-goat; the other
took one look, said 'Thambi, something's wrong.
This thing's iffy: cut its throat!'

Hearing this, the demon fled the pair
back to his lair
where the gibing of his pals around the fire

got his blood up, and before
you could say, 'the events of Black July, 1983',
his mob were out for an eye for an eye,

beating, flames in hand, at Able-Talker's door.
Which stayed locked tight. But through it
floated the loud, theatrical

voices of that smart bluffer and his wife:
'What became of those three demons in the larder?'
—'Our little boy's bedtime snack!'

If a child devoured three of their kind,
the parents would eat thousands! So the mob fled,
leaving that Tamil home unlooted and unburned.

Next time

it's said, with that infuriating head-shrug
—acquiescent jocund
wobble, figure of eight—
or with a sniff-kiss of my scalp

EVERYTHING HAPPENS FOR A REASON

—I won't fight it. I won't cite
casualties of the war or tsunami,
innocents in prison, nor incendiarists
closer to home.

EVERYTHING HAPPENS FOR A REASON

said that courtier—a Tamil Leibniz
even when the king by accident
sliced with a letter-opener his own pinky off
and locked our man up for those words.

A year later, while hunting,
said king
was captured by those
seeking a sacrifice to their god:

seeing his lopped hand—impure!—
they let him go. And so
the king set the courtier free:
'I see now your wisdom.

But that year
you spent behind bars

at my command
—was that too written in the stars?'

Carefully, as—millennia hence—
his scion might ape
the Englishman's habit, of raising a pinky
while sipping tea,

his subject
replied: 'Were I, my lord, at large,
I would have accompanied your highness on the hunt,
been caught and killed...'

—Outspreading, like the wing-feathers of Garuda
ten flawless fingers!

Trinco

The flower they call firecracker
—*kanakambaram*
dances, is that the word (the mind blanks)
round the rebuilt pillars
made, like everything, of concrete
but painted to resemble
the wooden, once, walls that burned down
turning the house into the ghost of a house
bought for a pittance
(it was believed, too, that bodies were buried in the garden.)

The child who lives here now
pivots shyly, scratching
her ankle with her big toe;
everyone is bitten
all the time, there is always
the soft unconscious motion
of a hand, marking a pause of thought,
or when a question mustn't be answered,
breaking off to scratch an itch.

This ancient neighbour
sprinted, once,
across the giggling grass. Sixty years on
she and my mother, teeth unreally perfect
—dentures—grin stiffly.
Offering us a cold drink
she disappears. Minutes pass.
We go to the window. There she is,
picking oranges with a trembling hand,
callused heels rocking on the stepladder...

The juice arrives in gilt
rimmed tumblers and tastes
like soluble aspirin. 'You used to be so beautiful,'
she cackles, 'now you are fat!' Everyone
talks like this. They will never
see each other again. We don't stay long
—mind you don't trip, where like a snake
a blue hose winds through the path's pale sand.

Nanthikadal

Śaṅkara mentions the rope
left lying
on the path and mistaken
for a snake; ten
boys crossing a river,
of whom the last cries
'I see only nine,
we didn't all make it',
only to be
reminded that he,

himself, is the tenth; is god—

*

Toward pit latrines
and a few grains
of rice,
swim-wading
between one
set of murderers
and another,
a shot mother
dropped her baby
in the lagoon.

They also were god.

Burnt palmyra

Felling the other charred and telltale boles
turned black from brown and missing their crown
of leaves used to make baskets and hats,
and as paper by the ancient poets
whose works burned, with the rest
of Jaffna library; those leaves that were
turned into umbrellas as well, which may be why
when the shells came down on these
now cratered, lunar badlands
poor people hid beneath my boughs,
as if bombs might bounce off like rain...
Why is it those who took an axe to all
the scorched lopped trees that would
remember their crimes to the world
left me and me alone standing,
the voiceless lingam you drive past down
the tank-ruined road to the war museum
with its spalled propeller and piffling,
home-made submarines—arranged
to paint the Tigers as a joke
—where a troop of monkeys with a crash of leaves
leap along rusted, bathetic bulkheads
drooping apart in slices like carved meat?

Leaving Jaffna

everyone prays
at the Murugan kovil. A thumb
paints your brow
with thiruneeru,
vermilion,
sandalwood paste.

Later, you find yourself
sat on a
concrete block
at a table of concrete.
The place war widows run,
depending on no one:

paruppu, rice, bangles
of cuttlefish
afloat in bronze
கறி
—wild chicken,
more bone than meat.

May 2021

It won't go viral
but for a week
the X-Press Pearl's fumed slow
volcanic billows
—charcoal over blue-green

twenty-five personnel were airlifted to safety
the same number
of tonnes of acid
can never be extracted from the sea and its coral

it isn't moral

for centuries
the ocean
infested
with galaxies
of nurdles

here and now
lesioned turtles
blaze on the beach
next to a fish with plastic dentures

The elephant

—a grey, static shape
in the binoculars
whose neoprene strap
touches my neck unexpectedly, a brief, electric shock...

These jungle roads turn bittersweet. Is it
dusk's withdrawal
of those flaming colours, from bioluminescent grass
and the iron-rich red soil of Jaffna

or—Thomas Hardy's 'beauty of association', not of 'aspect'—
childhood memories resurfacing;
my parents slipping
obliviously into Tamil

in a room of brown, sweating strangers
while I kept that glum
unguarded look from glittering in my eyes,
plummeting without understanding

into that overflowing yet
prosodic tongue? The elephant
idles its trunk in some perplexity,
lured by dumped veg from the market

despite the fence of electrified wire
and the presence
of us and our parked hired van, also
the Buddhist monk who pulls his motorbike to

and steps onto the sand,
retrieving a camera from his saffron folds.
In the ancient chronicles, bloodstained
war elephants are compared to 'evening clouds'.

The elephant

in the room: stranger
everywhere you are, a spicy burp
of consciousness
—what's repeating on you?

One can't refuse Shakuni and his dice.

For years you've arisen
from sleep sad, complaisantly jocular, severed
from the, this moment
by a transgenerational bent
for abidance; separated from its object, fear is a poison
taken daily
in tiny sips—by now inhumanly tolerant
it is the saliva you swallow without thinking.

You are the elephant
in the elephant
orphanage, hunter-blinded, tall as a house:

at the heart of all your trying
immobile and cold
—year on year
there he was
chained to the banyan
hardly shifting
his trunk through the blazing reek, as if

to remind himself and the world quietly
he still lived—

Trinco

Egg hopper and sambal for breakfast and a glass of woodapple juice
whose reek one learns to block out, by concentrating,

for instance, on the hotel worker
pouring onto the pond fish food from a Coke bottle. Rioters

squatted, once, in the boughs of the shadowy mahilam
by the temple with its step of red tile

where the grandfather you never met used to sit and play
the harmonium. Beside the Shiva statue dancing to this day,

spoken of for years in your family. The god's
fingers and toes as frailly miraculous as a baby's;

his eyes have irises and pupils, even
you could lose yourself in the detail

of his snakelike hair, as in the leaping motions of fire.

A fisherman

walks inchmeal, like a child experimenting, along the sand. His head
is covered, there's a bag at his back and the net hangs like a hammock
between his readied hands. Is the sun, sea, sand, a painted backdrop;
shattering the simulation, will he see the world as it really is?

    As a child I cried and cried, and when no one came, pretended
that in the depths of my misery, with that eternal taste of tears in my
mouth, I had discovered at the crucial moment—like someone on
television—a flaw in the wallpaper or a misaligned book on the shelf, a
thread of some kind which when pulled, would unravel everything.

    Your anger

    at acts

        of appropriation

    is itself appropriative.

We wait and wait for the fisherman to throw his net, anticipating a
glorious shot of its shape against the sky. The sky in brilliant,
turquoise panes.

The last train

to arrive in Jaffna
during the war
30 years ago
rusts
on the tracks

the unimaginable
touch of time

has turned it
the colour, exactly
of this land's ferrous soil
—of blood that is

four men round a fire
purple smoke slants
upward—trunks
form the bier

The Annupoorunyamal

(or Florence C. Robinson)
—a scaled-down copy of a
'full rigged New England clipper';
or, 'a direct descendant
of an early
nineteenth-century British naval brig';
that Valvai thoni

plied long-known
Tamil sea-routes; made port
from Cochin to Vizhakapattinam, Aden to Rangoon;
carried rice, spice, tiles and timber
(sandalwood, teak),
tobacco and dried fish;
was purchased, for as much

paper money
as filled the back
'of an ancient open Buick';
sailed the Pamban Channel
to Colombo;
arrived in Gloucester, Mass., in August 1938:
her pilgrim crew,

'turbaned, beskirted', clomb the yards barefoot
—'a fine lot of men, too,
if you treated them right and respected their beliefs'—
singing 'lusty sea-chanties
in an in-
congruous'—fine word, *incongruous!*—
'biblical English'.

My mother's English

—rivering, glitch-thronged, dubitable, prodromal, gallionic, far-quarried, innocent of subtlety, narrowcasting, plethoric, spry, oysterish, unalleviated, pardonable, spicy, specious, spacious, toothless (literally), a biggish onslaught, a glassy envelope, heuristic, sanative, double-natured, word-incarcerated, burdensome, trophic, conciliatory, upended, bullied, marginal, bellied, managerial, belayed, belied, believed, beloved

Every year

they bought the safety-yellow panchāngam,
with its auspicious dates for a wedding,
advice on bulletproofing a journey
against acts of God;
how to breathe, and how to be forgiven; providing the meaning,
even, of a gecko falling from the ceiling onto your head.

It's all in your head.
My grandfather wanted more from the panchāngam.
He consulted horoscopes. He decrypted the meaning
of the jostling planets. An ayurvedic doctor, he gave—wedding
superstition and sincerity, refusing to be a god
to the poor—freely to those who made the journey

to his clinic—also my mother's home, the start of her journey.
She says I'm him, reincarnated. When his angina came to a head
his nitrate pills couldn't be found. There is only one god,
she says, and many paths, panchāngam or no panchāngam.
It was arranged, her wedding
to my father. The morning

after—as they breakfasted, that morning—
he ignored her, reading a book about a journey
into the dark heart of... A book for British boys. Did our wedding
mean nothing, she asked herself? He'd a good head
on him, but her father had a heart... Still, the panchāngam
declared their union auspicious. And she trusted in God.

And her husband, unlike others, didn't want her to see him as God.
Even as he corrected her English—her letters, her unmeaning
rote, spoken, phrases—she was his panchāngam,
guiding, making inevitable, their journey
to England. How else would the children get ahead?
Neither child would suffer a traditional wedding,

an arranged marriage. Our lives would be free verse. Or, a wedding
between impulse and form, desire and history, a dead god
presiding over it all... The dead live only in our heads.
Shrine-photos of Sai Baba have no, or the wrong, meaning.
My wife's name just fails to rhyme with 'journey'.
Where it didn't exist, we invented a panchāngam

dispersed into countless heads, meaning after meaning
multiplying like the limbs of gods. The cliché, of the journey...
Let us dance—as at our wedding—on the grave of the panchāngam.

Pillaiyar

—that's Ganesh to you—is pictured
with a broken tusk: why?

The tale was added
late on
to the *Mahabharata*.

Vyasa, author
requiring a scribe
asked that noble child with an elephant's head.

Only, replied the god,
if once begun we do not cease...
my pen mustn't rise from the page.

So the poem became
difficult: Vyasa improvised
knotty passages

Pillaiyar had to pause and parse
—while he, Vyasa, also took
a breath.
                 When the pen broke

Vyasa, as promised, kept unrolling
that wonderfully embroidered carpet of verse...
The elephant-god had no choice.

He snapped off his tusk,
dipped the end in ink and wrote with that.
Since then, all writing, everywhere, has this character.

It can't decide whether to speed up or slow down. It wants you
to understand. Then it plays hide and seek. There are two people here,
even before you arrive—playing tug-of-war.

Impulse and form. Breath and language.
And since the pen is a torn-out tooth
red between the lines

                          you'll taste blood

Lasantha Wickrematunge

So you've never heard of me—what happened
to looking up each and every
unfamiliar word? Instead of Googling yourself
or the outrage du jour
how about SRI LANKA WAR CRIMES
JOURNALIST ASSASSINATED—

My country has no museums of the dead.
No poppies and no wreaths
(except the one
killers sent my family before the act.)

This is a fact:
we delete graveyards,
palmyra trees shells
fired on civilians burned black.

Rather than look back
we build over tank-crunched tarmac
silk-smooth lanes flowing from lens to horizon.

Where outposts of barbed wire,
shrines of the wrong religion,
defaced good Buddhist soil,
we make a clean breast of it
—the dome of another stupa, pure white.

Be that as it may,
what have we here? A voice
living and dead, both me and not.

'So in my veins red life
might stream again, / And thou be conscience-calm'd'
—in the making of this poem, was no one harmed?
Journalists do things
otherwise. And there's Miguel Serveto:
—'I will burn, but this is a mere event;
we shall continue our discussion in eternity...'

My printed voice
rose from the grave:

> No other profession calls on its practitioners to lay down their lives
> for their art save the armed forces
> and, in Sri Lanka, journalism.

> Countless journalists have been harassed, threatened
> and killed. It has been my honour to belong to all those
> categories and now especially the last.

Some words have disappeared
as if snatched off the street and detained without trial
—who does this poet think he is?

The TID comes for you in a white van,
the poet with his white space; a blockhead
8000 miles from my bloodshed!

Look up what I really said.

Consider that Keats poem
there is no evidence
I ever read
—where the Ceylon
diver's ears gush blood
so the fountains of Europe pelt wealth.

Like finding in your back pocket
a rupee
or two you thought lost,
one discovers—in that, let's face it, 63
stanza test
of your wired attention span,
a phrase that glints like a shell-casing on Attidiya Road
or one of my headlines:
'two brothers and their murder'd man'
ride between realms
to the forest of death from the city of love.

The shifted adjective
foredooms Lorenzo dead-alive
and goes to show
between there and then and here and now
are strange bridges—moments
fusing places and events;
in your chest beats—my heart
and from my part
of the world rushes towards you
                              goods—and bads too...

Be that as it may
on Attidiya Road
the tourist may discover
my corpse in its silver Corolla.

I was stabbed in the temple;
men in black smashed the window
—I say stabbed
but a journalist must be exact;
their weapon wrapped
in newsprint has in fact

never been identified:
my crushed skull's tiny scars an inch apart suggest a cattle prod.

It is well known that I was on two occasions brutally assaulted,
while on another my house was sprayed with machine-gun fire.
Despite the government's sanctimonious assurances, there was
never a serious police inquiry into the perpetrators of these
attacks, and the attackers were never apprehended.

When finally I am killed, it will be the government that kills me.

I called out
the Tigers and government both.
I took no sides,
which in my country is not allowed
—money laundering,
abductions, ghost
companies, tsunami funds gone AWOL:
I exposed them all.

When the Tigers seized Palaly
the censor stepped in—still
I found a way. A Gordian NOT:

Heavy fighting was not raging in northern Jaffna peninsula and Tigers
were not pounding Palaly with heavy artillery and mortars for the
fourth consecutive day.

Tigers did not enter Kaithady on Wednesday night after 12 hours of
so-called fierce hand-to-hand fighting in which more than 40 soldiers
were not killed and scores not wounded.

Those soldiers in Kaithady,
alive and dead—unreal

as Schrödinger's cat, our pal Lorenzo
or my remains
'warm and capable' of a last editorial...

The free media serves as a mirror
in which the public can see itself
sans mascara and styling gel.

Yes, I said that.
But they killed my paper,
bought us out
(oh the good old days
when the press at Ratmalana was set ablaze
—one could fight fire
and not with fire).

Frederica Jansz
my brave successor
sent threats in red ink
had to leave the country

I've left too,
for here and nowhere else,
a citizen of your memory;
a citizen of this poem:

> *I want my murderer to know that I am not a coward like he is,*
> *hiding behind human shields while condemning thousands of*
> *innocents to death. What am I among so many? It has long*
> *been written that my life would be taken, and by whom.*

Those are my words:
this
is something else—

The Sri Lankan journalist Lasantha Wickrematunge, editor of *The Sunday Leader*, was likely assassinated. He wrote an editorial that, published after his death, stirringly accused his alleged murderers from beyond the grave. He received several awards posthumously, including the UNESCO World Press Freedom Prize.

Everything in italics was written by Wickrematunge. The editorial in question can be read online, but I'm also deeply indebted to *And Then They Came For Me*, a memoir by his widow, Raine Wickrematunge. In it she explains he once wrote a column appearing under the pseudonym 'Suranimala', which became famous for his catchphrase: 'be that as it may'.

I'm also grateful to members of the family for their kind responses to my poem. Minal Wickrematunge, Lasantha's niece, tells me that the exhumation revealed her uncle to have been shot with a cattle rifle.

Autumn

(after John Keats)

The fallen yellow leaves now oftener
flare red. Embers. Blown-up chilli-flakes.
The burning of the library at Jaffna.
Foreign dead about to break
the spell of here and now. Phantasms steal
into the peaceful lives we seem to have earned,
telling tales about what happened
to them, not us, and in a tongue I never learned.
This is my garden, my spade of blood meal
and from our kitchen the time-travelling smell
of chicken curry floats to Walden Pond.

—A swooping cardinal like a struck match.
Above the fence mosquitoes eddy
like opinion, crazed by a patch
of red-pink light into giddy
scribbling on the air. There is no need
to be ashamed. I see you there and keep
alive the thought of meeting one day
brightly after the next. Black mustard seed
thrums in the sauce, the sky falls asleep;
where feelings come from or may leap
across and through and to no one can say.

Tsunami-hit, shoved over at a tilt,
they've left the bashed old kovil's god-thronged tower
standing, tallish, beyond the new one built
to face, this time, becalm, the ocean's power...
Our autumn clouds are a far-quarried rubble
to which the changing light does spicy things.

To sing, to fly, migrate, are curious verbs;
beauty, like happiness, frailly reliable,
has nothing to do with why there are wings,
why birds build nests and sing their songs,
or why barbed wire's besotted with its barbs.

Mourning

(after Andrew Marvell)

What is the meaning of the tears
those mourning women in their shack
cried, or didn't, for—lost these years—
their children who did not come back:

grief unbegun and without end…?
Sri Lanka's a peculiar shape.
War-torn in two, it has remained
a single teardrop on the map:

Eelam, island within island
that no explosion could break free…
The sea-foam mingles with the sand,
the banyan's roots become the tree.

Unknowing is the utmost hell:
did her child die; or flee abroad?
Or is he tortured in a cell?
A mother's grief has been outlawed.

For how can she convey the news
to herself that her child is dead,
hope being a bomb she can't defuse
(her left wrist wears the sacred thread)?

Capsules on strings around their necks
—cyanide, in case of capture—
some longed to blow themselves up next
in lonely yet collective rapture.

The tears we cry, once separate,
become reciprocal; a sea
planes fly across; some emigrate:
my parents did, who made me me

—but I'm them too. They could not purge
that terror passed down like a gene.
Our histories can't but converge
for with a touch our griefs convene:

my mother's gifts of fear and dread
(as if some power still wants me dead)
wrote the meaning of a woman's pain
into these tears I can't restrain.

Sri Lanka

is every country
where I feel, and don't feel, at home

—a child,
leaving England
for Colombo's eerily
warm evenings and the alien
language of crickets,

I too was
fostered alike by beauty and by fear.

For many a year
through the doorway of dusk
I'd travel there.

'What's wrong?' someone might say
or, 'I love to see you smile';
but I was far away.

*

In lockdown with my wife and baby
in green Acton's
twilit warmth

I'm that lonely boy
listening for crickets
on a pink-tiled rooftop in Dehiwala.

*

What of this country
where I live now but should I leave
—if, say, the virus

touches my parents in England—
my visa may bar our return? Out
of caves in our garden's stone

wall peeps the immortal
squirrel I saw run
through ancient Polonnaruwa,

three white lines
burned into its back:
the fingermarks of Rama.

2020

Rama's bridge

That pebble in your shoe is the pebble
the squirrel rolled down the shore,
wishing like other, larger critters
to help the rescue effort. To build a bridge
'of wondrous strength / ...a hundred leagues in length'.

Fondly—was it a shade
patronising?—Rama, in gratitude,
stroked the squirrel's back.
His long, tapering, fingers of fire
branding its fur

with stripes lasting to this day. Unlike
that ghostly tombolo
visible from space: unstrung pearls
in a wash of phthalo and teal;
golden microbes still on the move.

Karna

till Frank fills his nappy—his diaper—
with the babble of scree
leaping down a mountainside

after he mouths that plinky sound
—a pebble dripped into Bashō's pond

he's inconsolable—big hot tussling
in my arms—then slow—an hour or more

my back aches like glass
a vein of light runs down my side
the feel of not to feel it Keats said

*

it's then I think
of Karna—the sun god's son
in the *Mahabharata*

should've been one of the heroes
grew up instead

a driver's son, insulted, driven
to rage against their undying light

do you know the story
he wanted the perfect weapon
the mantra of the sage Parashurama
would conjure
from the vacant air

—but the old man loathed
warriors of Karna's caste

so he lied
made himself—I've been there—unprepossessing
a simple hermit wishing only to learn

one day Parashurama
pillowed on Karna's lap
dozed off—imagine
those withered limbs, the moment
of white, slack hair, the face dark as a burned match—

*

I can't get over—beyond it—
that morning
my father creaked the door ajar
tiptoed in and told me
he was having a heart attack

not to worry—he, a doctor, had made the call—

I thought it was a dream
I fell back asleep

my mother arrived
went with him to the hospital
I stayed behind

with my wrongdoing and the exordium
to this dire this everlasting vigilance

it could have
happened—the worst thing—still could

and if he'd died

the old man who boasts of his strength
the old man who identifies
with Karna
—how could I go on
he'd have killed me too

*

Frank reactive—
prone
as the sunlit air
astral
with dead skin—star-stuff

our son named
for the detective who
has nothing to do
with that Sri Lankan city
though I mix up the spellings

What's your name?
    —*Columbo.*
Your first name?
    —*Lieutenant.*

How many of us—to be frank—
would escape that hectoring question
belong nowhere be nobody

but there's a little worm of self
that won't have it that simmers with grievance
this is why

the moment Frank goes to sleep in my arms—
round head slack, breathing even—

at once there develops
a crick in my neck
a spinal twinge
and worst of all
this itch at my right nostril

I've got to scratch   .

★

it's no good
my body its selfishness must
come first

—my parents
said I must succeed
go on forever
on their behalf and for the sake of all Tamils

how terrible to be a man
on a mission—I can't be still
the centre of the universe

how do I make it
all about him?

★

so there he was
cradling the old man
when a *worm* arose

it could mean *snake*—or prefigure
the arrow of Arjuna
that would end Karna's life

anyway the worm it crawled bloodily
not over but through his thigh
a flesh-tunnel—silent gore

staining his mendicant's robe, pale sand, the old man's hair
but Karna wouldn't budge
lest he wake the sage

*

meanwhile
Frank extends one hand
index finger and thumb

meeting as he sleeps
as if he were meditating

my pain drains away
turns into something
else—it's a miracle, I could stay
here forever, holding him, I know now
to not scratch is to win
to become immortal—a marble being—

I think of Heaney's poem about St Kevin and the blackbird

my father, refusing
to waken
me—and Karna—

*

kindness and pride
—my father experiences neither pleasure or pain
or so he says
it was my role in the family to have experiences
to represent—happy or unhappy
upholding our
immigrant endeavour

I was Krishna
doing my own epochal thing

that blue boy
ate earth
—his mother, when she prised his lips open
saw floating there and modelled in mud
the solar system or was it somehow
the real thing and no model?

*

who can understand
a selflessness that moves
beyond all reason
to the point of worshipping
its own rigour

or the secret
sunshine of that love

men shape between them
into unspeaking darkness

*

the sage awoke and saw
the blood—straightaway he knew
what had happened
and what's more

'you lied to me,' he said
'only a warrior—a *kshatriya*—would keep silent
through such terrible pain
only such a man
would be so needlessly brave
—you deceived me
and so I will teach you
the mantra but when you most need it
you will forget the words'

*

last night in his crib
Frank opened
his wet fresh-painted eyes

our golden child
has forgotten how to sleep
he thinks it involves screaming and kicking

it's enough to make you wonder
how does anyone do it

how do we cede ourselves how acquiesce
how does one line of a poem lead to another
how for the first time
does one say 'I love you'

one hand
a tiny moist starfish
searched the air
for a rung a presence which wasn't there

*

the gods made stick
Karna's chariot wheel
in the mud

so Arjuna could fire
arrows through his heart

Karna died softly on his belly
with a single tear glowing down his cheek
like Marion Crane in *Psycho*
—Frank when he gives up
on tummy time
turns his head to one side
still as the tomb
before his thumb finds his mouth or his mouth his thumb

Karna's heart
was protected once
by a radiant breastplate—the kavach he was born with

Indra, to set things in motion,
appeared in the form of a beggar

requesting politely
he tear it, pound of flesh and all, from his chest

for Karna could refuse nobody
in the dawn hours
that was one of his stupid macho rules

*

in this way the gods contrive everything
they pick the winners and losers
for even that detail about the stuck wheel of his chariot
was a little jab wasn't it
at how they'd torn from Karna his birthright
made him a driver's son

*

when I was a little boy
my father took me for drives

time together
I remember a flooded lane

rainy sunlit leaves—a cattlegrid—
happiness—

*

I lower Frank
to his mother's breast
his arms windmilling like Arbogast's
exhilarated fear

seeing the nipple
he reorients
like the saint in the *Stri Parva*
hung upside-down in a spiky pit
about to die—reaching out
for a taste of honey

what does Frank's
mixed skin
remind me of?

Trinco's Marble
Beach—maintained
by the airforce
—mournfully glowing

*

Karna learned the mantra anyway
—the charade
of struggling to remember

on the battlefield
the magic words—embracing
the myth he'd become

my father's back
was pierced by the sacred hooks
he danced in the dust with the kavadi on his shoulders

taking on, he said, our whole family's pain
but yes pleased to be looked at to be seen
grandiosely suffering

*

see that's what you call resentment

the ambivalence love can't shake
how terrible to think

Frank will both love and hate me
before and after I die

Karna should've guessed his provenance
in the daylight he felt good—the sun's son

come dusk he weakened in each mental sinew
for as Ramanujan tells us
every day is different

but night is ancient is immemorially the same

*

I don't want to
leave you in the dark

*

those days
before I
went to sleep
he—my father—
in a ritual hush
applied
holy ash
thiruneeru
to my forehead
with slow rubs

of his thumb—as one
might cherish
the tender button
between a woman's thighs

he whispered in rhythm
words beyond me
I stared at the ceiling and thought of England

afterwards
he kissed me on the mouth
on the unlit landing
and we embraced—one of us
standing, to make room,
a step above the other

My face

in the coffin-shaped hotel mirror
disquiets me now
we've returned from the temple
where my mother knelt and prayed and rose
so many times, circling
the crow-wild building
while faces dark as ours looked on.

'Everything,' she said, to reassure
this painted face in the mirror,
'will happen to you.'

(The priest's thumb
anointed my brow
with thiruneeru and sandalwood.)

A horse with an overt penis
leaped from the load-bearing pillar
of that Kali kovil with Kalis everywhere:
her paunch bulbous, teeth fangs;
morphed to a sinuous dancing girl;
bent backwards on reversed hands and feet, scuttling
along the ceiling like a Klein-blue spider…

(Unless I tell you otherwise
I am always tearing with my nail
at the skin of my keratinised thumb, leaving
panels of woebegone cerise.)

My grandfather's gravestone
is lost. 'Everything is gone,
but he was never there. Tomorrow
you will find him in his Sivan temple.'

Hillside temple

Schoolgirls in white blouses and with long, blue-black braids
stream down the road alive,
once, with dappled, leaping deer

—before they were shot by soldiers
like this bloke in his lucent boots
swaggering past the artillery centre

whose mural reads: 'WHEN THE GOING GETS TOUGH,
THE TOUGH GET GOING...' Fancying himself
an action hero walking in slow-motion

away from a coolly disregarded explosion
he leads the eye past the bars that keep
suicidal couples from Lovers' Leap,

where the sea's brilliant, soft-hard tremor
flashes a code through the boulder it's said
Ravana slashed with his sword.

Orts

isn't it strange

what we can be
harmed by;

what we think
may harm us;

our need
to give

harm
a local habitation
and a name?

how boring
that word *trauma* is

11 May 2022

According to —,
we shouldn't
while bombs fall on Ukraine
moot
issues of racial bias in
critical
writing

while Sri Lanka
is aflame

he has taken
the time
to write a letter
protesting
a letter on bias

that rented house in Wellawatte

everything
only
connected
by
ant ant ant

cold war

soft power
meant a nation
might give aid
because of
the allies—thereby—made;

being afraid
of migration
—all those brown
bodies washing up
on its own
shores

the moon

pale as thiruneeru
some real
meaty waves

irascible and tumid glints

thirukkural

to stand and speak among the learned
when you're without knowledge
is to play chess with half the pieces missing

but the knowledge
you think you possess
is always on loan

conception

when his tire-rod
gave out
my father noticed
by the side of the road
a small shrine to Pillaiyar
—just in case
it was the god
who saved him
from that day
on he never went that way
from Batticaloa to Trinco
in his Hillman Superminx

to court my mother
without pausing
to break
a coconut in gratitude

yes

'it is skill surmounting difficulty, and beauty
triumphing over skill'

the machete gleams
into xanthous exocarp

you suck the water out
and give the king

coconut back: with a stroke
it's halved

a spoon hewed
of its side

to scrape out the white flesh with

Travellers

(after Walter de la Mare)

'Is there anybody there?' asked the Soldier,
        Firing through the door,
And his Sam Browne belt glimmered
        In the sunlight's silent roar
As down the alley
        Of red earth they fled
—My uncle and auntie and granny:
        'Is there anybody there?' he said.
Though neither *asked* nor *said* is the word
        For the sound of his mouth or his gun.

In the dead of night to that sunlit house
        I return, testing with my finger
Each hole a bullet made;
        Until I cannot linger
Longer, hearing from the other side
        The gunshot of a knock
At that vanished door
        I rush to unlock. Ghosts step out
Into the foreign air:
        People who, wherever they are, are,
Like me, not all there.

During the rioting of 'Black July' in July 1983—when Sri Lankan Tamils were killed—soldiers fired through the front door of my uncle's house. The whole family, including his mother—my grandmother—leapt the fence before returning to their trashed home the next day. Two years later, the family fled to India, knowing they'd be targeted.

Eelam

If my parents were, are, nervy,
camouflaged—against carnivory;

if, at day's end, their choice is
a belief in perpetual crisis;

if this autotomy and playing dead
(a jettisoned tail, ink squirted)

is the only language they
felt it safe to bequeath;

then, to smile today
with unclenched teeth,

to sleep well, not brood—an ingrate—
over trivially frictive grit

till the pearl of nightmare is fished;
to be *at peace*—wouldn't this

betray my parents and my dead,
dismiss as nullity all they did?

Research

The lawn's frozen-over snow
gleams evilly, like polystyrene.
A foot plunged in it to the knee
might as well
have been cancelled from existence,
dissolved into aching particles. As if
that aspect of the universe that has evolved,
in the form of my person,
to the point of wondering at itself
collapsed back into the void that is Brahman.

'I don my mask before exiting the car'
—no longer merely
an MFA-ish first sentence...
Every piece of large, bluish grit on the platform
deserves a platform. Has its shadow. You too
should read Tamara Fernando's essay
on the pearl-fisheries of Mannar.
What wás a paar?
I ask myself every day. Sunday
was like summer

—a Sri Lankan summer—
something isn't right. 'Sometimes
oysters settled amidst seagrass
[...]
they seemed to live
happily alongside starfish and turtles;
at other times the latter swallowed up
the entire bed.' You wouldn't believe
through the window
these brumal golden climes.

(What Orwell said
about prose
is always on my mind.) The mask needs adjusting.
Blood sprang
from diverse nostrils. Divers'. There
is something in my shoe.
Every step reminds me. A particle
whose etiology I could explore, in another article
—no more. Is it you, walking a mile?
I wish you'd stop.

Jaffna, January 15, 2023

From the shop-shack—years ago—
at the Kanniya hot wells
I purchased a soft dark hat, my father vetoing the camo-pattern.
Trees entwined, rough bark and smooth.

Disrobing, our driver
sauntered through the glittering crowd
of Hindus and Muslims and Christians,
past a child doused by its parents

with the healing volcanic water,
shampooed, even
—occupying a space
between a woman in hijab and a priest's soaked soutane.

＊

Water cannon at Jaffna—no *s*, in my English—
Tamils pulled out bottles of shampoo,
washing the regime
right out of their hair.

＊

A soldier yelled 'ticket'.
Ananthan—it means *the smiling one*—
rebuttoned his damp shirt. Drily
my father emptied his pockets;
but the man with the rifle
meant only,
did we want to enter the raffle…?

*

'Had I not seen several China merchants
shampooed before me, I should have
been apprehensive...'
—From the Hindi, *čāmpo*: to press.

The Star of India

blanked by unending rivers
of foot-traffic

traipising from diorama to dinosaur
between vivarium and gift shop

—misnamed. A billion or two
years in the mineral depths

of our teardrop
island (they weren't spent

waiting on J.P. Morgan)
moved to radiant union

its milky tendrils
like the dendrites of a neuron.

O
blue-grey cabochon

the colour of my dead
grandmother's cataract!

As a child

because my voice was not the right voice
and could not be understood I stood
before the *mirror*—a murky glassen word
this mouth can't shape right to this day—and was made
to watch my teeth and lips being imprecise.
So this is why I come across a Southron
and not from Yorkshire, or Sri Lankan; but I'll complain
no more about this clarified and potent tongue

for when the moustached gent at US Customs
asked me in his hapless twang
are you a terrorist, my borrowed posh it sure
abashed that poor colonial; and it was of course
what my child-face perceived or could not in the glass
which made of me a scrutineer of sound,
a listener for and into every glitch
in the aathma, the script, the avid void of English.